Professional Development Series
Volume Two

An Introduction to Archives and Manuscripts

David B. Gracy II
Director
Texas State Archives

Mary Frances A. Hoban
Series Editor

Special Libraries Association
New York, New York

Library of Congress Cataloging in Publication Data

Gracy, David B.
   An introduction to archives and manuscripts.

   (Professional development series ; v. 2)
   Bibliography: p.
   1. Archives. 2. Archives--Management.
I. Title. II. Series.
CD950.G7   025.17'1   81-5677
ISBN 0-87111-288-4   AACR2

Table of Contents

Introduction

On History tests, I used to ask students to identify and explain the significance of various events and terms. Invariably I would include the term "archives" in the list. The answers usually parroted one or more of the three meanings of the word.

First, "archives" are the noncurrent records of an organization or institution preserved because they possess information of permanent value. These days the word "information" is underscored. Data today are generally considered more important than the particular medium on which they are recorded. This is a rather recent trend, sparked by the incredible volume of records produced during the twentieth century. Archives come into existence to facilitate and record the activity of organizations as they conduct their business. Archives are not created to be archives. After the files have fulfilled their original purpose, and largely because they fulfilled that purpose, those of permanent value become archives: our documentary heritage, our recorded memory of ourselves.

Second, an "archives" is the agency in which archivists work. Their work consists of several related but distinct activities: accessioning, appraisal of historical value, arrangement, description, conservation and restoration of the physical document, and reference. Oral history projects, publications, and exhibits spice and supplement many archival programs. But were the archivist pressed to say which of these were the bedrock of archival work, which the professional archivist is specially trained to do, the answer would come quickly: appraisal, arrangement, description, and reference.

The third definition of "archives" is the building housing the agency.

Of all the answers on the tests, one was different from the rest. Its author scrawled: "Archives are places where records of the past are kept for reference in the future, if necessary." In a society as litigious as ours, a society clearly in the Age of Information, a society that sends more genealogical researchers into libraries than plain readers, the question no longer is whether to keep records. The question has become: "how?" and "how well?"

The goal of this introduction to archival work is to review the philosophy underlying the chief features of archival methodology. In the section titled "Principles," we review the basic facts that govern archival work, and consider the ramifications of each of these axioms. What archival work is, how it is done, and how it compares with and differs from librarianship are the themes addressed throughout. The section on "Procedures" lays out the course of archival work and describes general practices.

The difficulty in writing something this short, of course, is the danger of generalization. Sometimes concepts must be presented too directly, too simply. Everyone with experience in an archives knows that little in the work is cut and dried, black and white. Everyone with experience in a library knows things are not as monolithic as they may seem to appear in these pages. The comparisons herein are drawn only to illustrate points. Of course, there are always exceptions. Always one more example would have clarified the nuances of a broad statement. Partly to meet these objections, a bibliography of readily available books, pamphlets, and articles concludes this booklet.

Special thanks go to Jean Carefoot, Charles Hughes, David Murrah, Mike Hooks, Helen Clements, Chris LaPlante, Carolyn Majewski, Michael Dabrishus, Audray Bateman, and Mary Hooper Bell for their critical reading of the manuscript.

Glossary of Selected Terms*

Accession—(1) The act and procedures involved in a transfer of legal title and the taking of records or papers into the physical custody of a repository. (2) The materials involved in such a transfer of custody.

Archives—See the three definitions in the Introduction. When the term denotes records, it is usually reserved for records actually in the repository. Thus the archives of the United States Government are those files in the National Archives. Records bound for the National Archives are just "records" until they arrive. Many persons conscious of the lack of a corresponding word for the papers of individuals and families stretch "archives" to include them.

Archivist—(1) The professional who works with archives (def. 1). (2) All who work in the field of appraising, obtaining, arranging, describing, and referencing of permanently valuable records, archivists and curators alike.

Collection—(1) In the informal, but more commonly used sense of the word, an archival record group in the hands of—collected by—an institution other than the archives (def. 2) of the creator. In a historical manuscripts repository, a body of papers is also often casually styled a "collection." Various institutions, university archives in particular, collect record groups of other creators and papers to provide materials for research by academics, genealogists, and others. (2) The formal sense of the word (spelled with a capital C) means documents arbitrarily assembled, such as the autographs of signers of the Declaration of Independence, to serve a purpose other than documenting the person or organization whose papers the documents once were a part. Curators of manuscripts repositories used to create Collections around various themes, but have abandoned the practice as destructive of the integrity of the record groups and papers from which the various documents came.

Creator—The person or organization that produced a body of papers or records in the course of living and conducting business. The term is not applied to the assembler of a Collection (def. 2).

Curator—The professional who works with records and papers in a historical manuscripts repository.

Document—Any discrete item, whether printed or manuscript, whether a report, letter or photograph, whether produced by a government agency, business, or individual.

---

*Several of the definitions have been drawn directly from Frank B. Evans, et.al., "A Basic Glossary For Archivists, Manuscript Curators, and Records Managers," *American Archivist.* 37 (July, 1974), 415–434.

Files—A collective term usually applied to all records of an office or agency, and occasionally to the papers of an individual. The term implies the presence of a system and device (such as a folder) in which the records and papers are organized. Additionally the term is used to designate a group of file folders, usually when holding records of common origin or subject.

Finding Aids—The descriptive media, published and unpublished, created by an originating office, an archival agency, or manuscript repository, to establish physical, administrative and/or intellectual control over records and other holdings. The most common finding aids include inventories, annotated lists, guides, and indices.

Historical Manuscript Collection—(1) A collection of papers or records of enduring value. (2) A repository that collects, holds, and makes collections available for research.

Manuscript Collection—See: Collection; Historical Manuscript Collection.

Manuscripts—(1) Single documents. (2) Drafts of a literary work. (3) One or more collections (def. 1)—in essence all nonarchival material.

Noncurrent Records—Records no longer consulted with any regularity by their creator in the course of business.

Papers—The archives of individuals and families. These bodies of material are quite different from organization records because they rarely exhibit the same careful structure, their contents normally are more varied and require extensive work to prepare for research use, no law mandates their existence or disposition, and of course their personal nature requires the archivist to be especially mindful of legal entanglements in their acceptance and use. Like the word "records," the term "papers" is used both when referring to all and to part of the files of the creating person or family.

Provenance—(1) In general archival and manuscript usage, the "office of origin" of records, e.g., that office or administrative entity that created or received and accumulated the records in the conduct of its business. Also the person, family, firm, or other source of personal papers and manuscript collections. (2) Information of successive transfers of ownership and custody of a particular manuscript or group.

Record Copy—The one copy of a document selected for permanent preservation. Normally it is the original, but if the original is lost, it may be a copy.

Record Group—The records of a distinct organization held by an archives. If the files are not too voluminous, all the records of the organization are called a Record Group. For utility and convenience in cases in which the archives of an organization are very voluminous, the records of various independent, or at least distinct, administrations (office, bureau, agency) are designated Record Groups. For example, the files of the Headquarters of the Army constitute one Record Group. In this case, there is no single term for the body of records produced by the entire United States

Army. The term is used more commonly in the archives of the creator than in a manuscripts repository.

Records—The files, whatever their form—paper, machine readable, or visual materials—created by organizations in the transaction of their business. The word is used in referring to parts of a record group, and with a capital R as a synonym for record group. Thus minutes are records found among the Records of the Hydrographic Office.

Security Copy—A duplicate copy, usually on microfilm, of records. Normally these are housed in a different location from the original copy so that in case of a disaster one copy would survive.

Series—File units or documents arranged in accordance with a filing system or maintained as a unit because they relate to a particular subject or function, result from the same activity, have a particular form, or because of some other relationship arising out of their creation, receipt, or use.

Subgroup—A body of related records within a record group, usually consisting of the records of a primary subordinate administrative unit. Subgroups may also be established for related bodies of records within a record group that can best be delimited in terms of functional, geographical, or chronological relationships. Subgroups, in turn, are divided into as many levels as are necessary to reflect the successive organizational units that constitute the hierarchy of the subordinate administrative unit or that will assist in grouping series entries in terms of their relationship.

Subseries—An aggregate of file units within a series readily separable in terms of physical class, type, form, subject, or filing arrangement.

The Principles

Archival Work Is Archival Work

Similarities in the work of archivists and of those professionals most often identified as close relatives to archivists—librarians and historians—are easy to spot and important to recognize.* Archivists and historians share a strong interest in the preservation and enjoyment (use) of history. Archivists and librarians share a commitment to promote the flow of information. All three work with our priceless documentary heritage, and the importance of the partnership cannot be over-emphasized. Each, however, fills a need not met by the other two and therefore has a unique role to play.

A prominent historian once quipped that an archivist was simply a historian with good housekeeping habits. There is a kernel of truth in the statement. However, where history begins, archival work leaves off. Archivists prepare records for use; historians use them. The archivist's intellectual contact with the body of records consists first of assessing its historical value, second of relating and ordering the various items and groups of items within it, third of describing both the whole and the parts, and finally of assisting patrons in locating files that contain information pertinent to their research. The historian, on the other hand, employs the information in the files both to tell a story and to test a hypothesis. One chore is primarily administrative, the other expository. Certainly, a good archivist could be a good historian, and vice versa. But the two roles are distinct and in pursuing them the individual punches two separate clocks.

The differences between archival work and librarianship on the surface appear small. After all, both use buildings of similar design, similar shelving and reading rooms. Both are administrative activities. Indeed, the majority of archival repositories in the United States are divisions of libraries. Yet the differences between the two are real. They spring from the nature of the material in the two types of repository and the treatment given it.

Papers and records are the documentary residue of activity—administrative remains. Books result from conscious research, study, thought, and the work of writing done for the purpose of informing and entertaining—a cultural endeavor. Archivists handle papers in groups formed around their creator; librarians treat each volume as an individual and separate item. Records impose their preexisting order on the archivist, while the librarian imposes a preexisting classification system on the books. Subject cataloging,

---

*Records managers are so closely related professionally that often they and archivists are mistaken for each other. Precisely because the relationship is so close, they are not included here. References to records management will be found throughout the pages that follow.

so central to librarianship, plays virtually no role in archival endeavor. Two distinct methodologies flow from these differences. Mixing them, like crossing two live wires, risks violating the integrity of papers and records, thereby causing irretrievable loss of information.

Because of the inherent differences among the archival, library, and history professions, the training appropriate for any one cannot give adequate preparation for work in the others. Neither librarianship nor archival work prizes the historian's proficiency in research, writing, and teaching. The techniques of appraisal are superfluous to the work of both librarians and historians. The list could continue. But the point is clear that all three are separate and distinct fields with equally separate and distinct methodologies.

Archivists Think "Groups"

The basic unit with which an archivist works is a body of records—not one document or item, but a body of records.

Archivists did not elevate groups to their primacy by chance. The oldest axiom in the archivist's portfolio is "Respect des fonds"—respect for the integrity of the group. The concept arose in the 1840s in France in reaction to an unfortunate situation. Prior to the French Revolution, government records, current and noncurrent together, stayed in the offices that created and used them. There was no national archives, as we know it, before the new leaders of France opened the records to the inquiring eyes of the citizens. The French Revolution revised the ancient tradition of government files maintained solely for government use, rather than for the people. Appreciating the archives more for their age than their administrative utility, scholars replaced government administrators in charge of the records. Of course the scholars brought their own tradition of organizing material around subjects of study, not unlike the classification system of a modern library. After forty years, however, the system collapsed under its own weight.

The effort to divide the records of one office into various arbitrary categories proved tedious, inexact work. Often several topics were covered in one document, but the document could go into but one place. Some researchers inevitably found the classifications unsuited to their inquiries. Moveover, it was extremely difficult to establish the continuity of work of any one office, and the transfer of modern records proved difficult. Out of this experience, and the subsequent reassertion of the role of the administrator in working with records, grew the principle that groups of records should be protected as groups. This concept still guides archival thinking today.

The importance of the group—the framework—drives to the heart of the difference between archives and libraries. Classification of a book does not, nor is it intended to, provide the patron a context for understanding or appreciating the contents of the volume. It merely serves to aggregate books on similar subjects as a convenience for locating them. Archival arrangement and description, on the other hand, clarify the internal relationships of all units within a single body of records.

Actually, an archivist has much in common with an automobile mechanic. Both work with units made up of many individual parts—cars for the one, record groups and collections for the other. They receive the units usually in a state of disrepair or disarray. Their jobs are to tinker with the units, or those subunits that most need their attention, until, for the mechanic, all the parts are in proper relation to each other, tuned, and balanced. The archivist has completed the chore when the records and papers are arranged and described adequately to facilitate locating on demand the information they hold.

While an auto mechanic being shown a disabled vehicle asks first: "What's wrong?" an archivist confronting a pile of records or papers wants to know: "What is the unifying thread that characterizes it, that makes it a unit?" Usually the common denominator is the person or organization that created the records or papers—the "creator." The nature of the individual items within the collection is a secondary consideration. Whether they are letters or books, financial accounts or deeds, minutes or case records; whether their subject is politics or social events; both or neither; whether they were written by figures of world renown or by persons unknown; whether they are old or young—all these are important considerations, but never the first one.

Having said this, no one would claim that the usefulness of archives is confined strictly to documenting events for the creator. Employed by a public relations department in developing an advertising campaign, or by a historian preparing a company history, or by a genealogist searching a family tree, archives serve a different, but equally valid use. The important and interesting point is that even this research use by second parties profits from the group context established by the creator.

A single letter may be complete unto itself. But its meaning is amplified when the item is seen in relation to the letter it answers, the answer it evokes, and the entire file of which it is but one part. We can extend the comparison of archivists and mechanics by comparing archives to cars. Both are made up of many parts, all of which have meaning and work in relation to each other. One letter, or one car door is useful, but not nearly as much as when placed in context in its body of records or attached to its car.

Often archivists find files labeled "Historical Material" or "History" proudly maintained as the archives of an organization. And they cry. The context is gone, the tree is stripped of its bark. Are the documents in the file official? From what office? What records are missing? How comprehensive is the file? The context is gone.

Both the archivist and the researcher seeing a document for the first time can know something about it simply by knowing in what group it is located, by knowing what office or person created it. The president of a business performs one set of duties, the production manager another, the financial officer yet a third. Their records reflect those differences.

The group concept even figures in seeking and appraising material for permanent preservation. The archivist looks for material in groups, and if offered a few documents in a "history" file, always probes to find out from which files these items were extracted. Similarly, in considering a group for permanent preservation, the archivist weighs the group as a whole before looking at the individual items as individual items. And if the group has value, often documents are retained within it whose information, of little value alone, is unlocked by virtue of the data in other documents.

There Is a Difference Between Archives and Manuscripts

Archivists distinguish between two kinds of groups—archives and manuscripts. The dichotomy is based upon the nature and purpose of the institution that holds the records and the use that is made of the files.

The history of this division stretches back nearly two hundred years to the decision of the Massachusetts Historical Society to collect historical documents—records and papers other than the operating files of the Society. The term "manuscripts" may have first been applied to this material because so many of the early accessions were single documents, such as letters, diaries, and actual literary works, appreciated as the literary remains of a particular individual. Hundreds of institutions, principally historical societies and libraries, have followed the Society in accumulating papers, records, lone documents, and ephemera from all manner of sources: well-known and obscure persons, prosperous and defunct companies, those who created the records and those who collected them. The unifying thread through all of these accessions was that none were official records of the collecting institution. A methodology heavily influenced by library procedures grew up for arranging and describing those materials.

The sheer bulk of papers created by individuals and organizations in our time, however, is causing manuscripts repositories to adopt and adapt principles of work with archives, principles designed for managing large, organic groups. Where special libraries that worked with records used to be concerned primarily with acquiring and servicing manuscripts for research and antiquarian interest, they are now more frequently called upon to control the records problem of their own organizations. This means, or should mean, establishing and maintaining an archival program.

The difference between archives and manuscripts is more than a matter of semantics. It begins with the functions they serve: archives are maintained primarily for their administrative usefulness to the creating organization, while manuscripts are kept for cultural and educational purposes, that is, for study and research. This fundamental difference is reflected in the way the two bodies are treated.

The method of acquisition, for example, is, or should be, different. Archives (records) should come to the archives (repository) in an orderly way either directly from the offices where the records are created, if the organization is a small one, or through a records management system.

Archives thus remain the property of the organization. Manuscripts, on the other hand, must be sought out by the curator. Often elaborate programs are established to help the curator learn about and then acquire manuscript collections. When a collection changes hands physically, legal title should pass as well.

The size of a unit of archives—record group, subgroup, series, and subseries—usually is significantly greater than that of a comparable unit of manuscripts. Organizations simply create more voluminous records. Hence archives require more space for their permanent preservation than do manuscripts.

On the other hand, manuscripts, though of lesser volume, require more work in arrangement and description than do archives, because individuals normally are not so meticulous in ordering and preserving their papers as are organizations with their records. Curators can expect to devote more hours to establishing order within a collection than is necessary for a record group of comparable size. More time is necessary, too, for the production of finding aids, since any researcher has less of an idea of the contents of a manuscript collection—for example the Arthur P. Duggan Papers in the Southwest Collection at Texas Tech University—than of an archival record group, such as the Records of the Adjutant General of Texas in the State Archives. A poor job of describing the adjutant general's office records will place a hurdle in the path of their use, but the same poor job on the Duggan Papers will erect a barrier obscuring the unique information in them until a patron comes along with the fortitude to take the extra time necessary to find the data locked inside.

Archivists Work With Unique Materials

Papers and records are the literary and intellectual fingerprints of their creator. Every record group and collection is one-of-a-kind, because no two persons or organizations are the same, operate during the same period, have identical interests, go about things in the same way, or maintain the same quantity and quality of records. Each group is singular, too, because the individual items that make it up are unique. This is true especially for records predating the invention of the photocopy machine in the latter half of the twentieth century, and even more particularly predating the use of the typewriter at the end of the nineteenth century. Few individuals went to the trouble, or even had the inclination, to make copies of handwritten letters. Governments and businesses made copies in various ways, but where simple hand copying prevailed, the copy often varied from the original in several details. Thus even the copy could become a singular document.

In our own age of duplication by carbon paper, print, and photocopy, the archivist pressed for space has had to become aggressive in assuring that only the unique document finds a place on his shelf. Thus arose the concept of the *record copy*. This normally is the original of a document. If only copies survive, the archivist selects one to serve as the record copy within the record group, or perhaps for the entire archives (repository). Usually all other copies are discarded in order to conserve precious space.

Sometimes records take strange forms. A local historical society once received a collection containing genealogical data recorded on popsicle sticks. The staff of a state archives found a note received by the state police on a paper collar of the type worn in the 1880s. In these cases, the archivist weighs the intrinsic value of the form of the document against the informational value (see page 21) of the data it contains to determine the best way to keep it. In the historical society, the popsicle sticks were placed on a photocopy machine and their data transferred to 8½×11 inch sheets more easily handled. The state archives, on the other hand, left the collar as it was, both for display purposes and because the nature of the file was such that little danger was posed to the physical safety of the item.

The fact that each record group and collection is the only one of its kind in existence places demands upon an archivist beyond those incumbent upon other professions that handle information. The contents of a volume require no arrangement by a librarian, and little in the way of description. The basic bibliographical entry, plus several added entries revealing the major topics or themes of the book, is all that the cataloger need produce. Records managers have little concern for contents, arrangement or description beyond that provided by the creator, since they store the records only temporarily, and then strictly for the use of the office.

The archivist, by contrast, looks forward to verifying the accuracy and efficiency of an arrangement or to creating an organization from scratch if need be. Whatever the body of records lacks to unlock its information for the would-be user, this the archivist must create. The work is no small order for a collection or record group containing more than a few documents.

Since each body of records is unique, no description of one will fit any other. Even where two repositories have original papers produced by the same creator, the holdings will not be identical. (If they are, one repository or the other must be wasting space.) Thus archivists do not, and never will, have the concept of cooperative cataloging. Any data on collections they enter into or receive from a data bank like OCLC is strictly for purposes of information. This means, too, that it is incumbent on archivists to spread information on their holdings. Hence they produce guides to describe the contents of individual repositories. Hence, too, the archival community emphasizes national accumulations of information such as the *National Union Catalog of Manuscript Collections* compiled at the Library of Congress and the *Directory of Archives and Manuscript Repositories in the United States* produced by the National Historical Publications and Records Commission.

Finally, appreciating the uniqueness of every body of records, archivists feel a special obligation to assist those who come to use the holdings. Explanation of the finding aids in a repository generally is not service enough for patrons to be able to make full use of all the holdings likely appropriate to their research. Archivists expect to assist researchers also by helping to relate the topic of their study to the organization and arrangement of the material in which relevant information may be found.

Archivists Keep Order

The next great discovery, following establishment of the principle that groups should be kept together—respect des fonds—was that documents within groups should be maintained in the order in which the office filed them.

The French, who introduced respect des fonds in reaction to the practice of fragmenting existing record groups, did not abandon the idea of segregating records among various predetermined, arbitrary topics. Within each group they continued to classify and file records by subject. And they continued to reap the whirlwind.

Officials needing to use their old office records chafed at the system that scrambled documents from offices within an agency. Hence in the 1880s the precise Prussians established the principle that records should be filed in the order of their origin. This Principle of Provenance, coupled with respect des fonds, stands today at the core of archival procedure and directs that, within their groups, records be kept in the order established by the creator—their original order.

Through the years the benefits of maintaining the original order have been widely appreciated. For the creator, a familiar arrangement facilitates officials' use of their own noncurrent records. For the repository, preserving the original order demands the least work. Where a filing system is unchanged, the integration of newly received files with existing holdings in the archives is readily accomplished. Moreover, revising an order is a very big task. Any change, however slight, worked all the way through a record group or collection of any size—for example converting a file arrangement from chronological with the most recent document at the beginning (which is the way many offices set up their files) to chronological with the oldest document first (the way historians prefer)—can be a herculean task consuming substantial staff time.

Finally, to the researcher, preservation of the original order, rather than arbitrary division of the documents into classes, obscures no information available to the creator of the files. After all, if the personnel in the office could locate data in the files, there is no reason a researcher cannot do the same. Moreover, study of the order in which an organization maintained its files frequently yields insight into the nature and functioning of the organization.

Order in a body of papers runs both vertically and horizontally. Vertically there are five levels of arrangement, beginning with the document as the smallest unit and first level. Second, a group of documents brought together for convenience in filing, is a file unit. The most common file unit today is a folder of loose documents. The relation of documents in a file unit is determined largely by the characteristics of the individual documents: their date and the quantity that could be placed conveniently in a folder. The third level, the series, is distinguished by attributes of the records as a body. The file units and documents that make up a series are maintained as a unit because they relate to a particular subject or function, result from the same activity, have a particular form, or have a relationship rooted in their creation, receipt or use. The series is the most important level in vertical order and arrangement, for it is here that the character of the record group or collection is established. The record group/collection, the fourth level, is the plane on which the principle of respect des fonds applies. On the final level—the repository—arrangement is governed by convenience in retrieval and guided by the desire to avoid shifting the location of holdings any more than necessary.

Across the collection and record group, the archivist can arrange the documents and files in one or more of three ways. Ordering by chronology is almost always used at the document level, frequently at the folder level, very rarely at the series level, and almost never as the framework for organizing an entire body of material. Another form of horizontal order is type of material. "Type of material" is a generic description of a document regardless of its date or subject. The ten types, along with some of the principal kinds of documents within each, are listed on the following page. Probably the least used horizontal arrangement is alphabetical order. While on the document level, arrangement of items by author is readily accomplished, division by subject or topic is not. First, nomenclature frequently must be determined. Is a topic to have the contemporary appellation "consumption," or the modern "tuberculosis"? (Usually the contemporary term is preferred.) A more basic concern, in a document that discusses more than one subject, as most old letters and many modern ones do, is under which subject should the item itself be filed? Which subject is the most important? Instead of making that decision, archivists believe their task to be establishing an arrangement and description that will readily expose to the potential reader, whatever his inquiry, the nature and extent of the information in the body of material. They believe, too, that making photocopies to insert into the files at likely points is an unacceptable practice. It wastes space, and worse, violates the integrity of the records.

Archivists Leave Trails

Archivists leave two kinds of trails. One follows each body of material in the repository from accessioning through processing. Along the other the researcher finds information about the contents of the papers and records themselves.

For every accession, the archivist creates two records. In an accession book each body of material is entered for ready reference and assignment of

CHECKLIST OF TYPES OF MATERIAL

*CORRESPONDENCE
  **Letters
  Greeting cards
  Telegrams
  Letter books

DIARIES, MINUTES, PROCEEDINGS
  Commonplace books

PRINTED MATERIAL
  Certificates
  Awards
  Pamphlets
  Brochures
  Proofs
  Circulars
  Flyers
  Clippings
  Broadsides
  Programs

FINANCIAL DOCUMENTS
  Ledgers
  Journals
  Bank statements and checks
  Bills and receipts
  Notes

PHOTOGRAPHIC MATERIAL
  Positive transparency
  Positive print
  Negative print
  Movie film
  Video tapes

LITERARY PRODUCTIONS
  Research notes
  Manuscripts
  Reminiscences
  Memoirs
  Reports
  Speeches
  Sermons

LEGAL DOCUMENTS
  Contracts
  Petitions
  Agreements
  Briefs
  Depositions
  Insurance policies
  Wills
  Inventories of estates
  Mortgages
  Deeds
  Abstracts of title

**SCRAPBOOKS AND
  SCRAPBOOK MATERIAL**

**MAPS, CHARTS,
  DIAGRAMS, GRAPHS,
  LISTS, ETC.**

AUDIO RECORDINGS
  Wax discs
  Audio recording tape

*General types are capitalized.
**Specific types listed are but the more common documents within the larger category.

From David B. Gracy II, *Archives and Manuscripts: Arrangement and Description* (Chicago, 1977).

accession numbers. Simultaneously, all documents preceding and arising out of the transaction are accumulated in an accession file. Important as the archivist's full record of the accession, the file can also be essential to a researcher needing a history of the body of material to validate the authenticity or official character of the files. In time, the accession file will include records of the work done on the material in the repository. In the short term, such records insure that the necessary work is accomplished; in the long term, they provide data that can be useful if a subsequent accession needs to be added to the collection.

The inventory is the backbone of the archivist's descriptive program for researchers. Each inventory describes a single body of records or papers. Often printed for distribution outside the repository, as well as for use within, this stocktaking reveals the collection or record group primarily by its series and subseries.

For the researcher in the repository seeking information likely to appear in more than one collection or record group, many archivists create annotated lists and indices. Since research use of records demands that as many avenues as possible lead to the information in the files, those who create annotated lists and indices rarely establish a subject list or index alone. Most add a chronological list or index. Some maintain cards also for geographical regions, for autographs, and/or for types of material, such as diaries.

For the potential researcher unaware of the repository's holdings, archivists produce a guide. Printed for wide distribution, a guide provides one or two uniform and descriptive paragraphs detailing the contents of each body of records in the archives. These volumes are produced only after a repository has accumulated fairly broad and substantial holdings. Often they are viewed as testimony that a repository has reached maturity.

Every Repository Is Unique (and Must Be Treated Accordingly)

First, every body of papers and records a repository holds is one-of-a-kind. No two repositories ever can have the same holdings, nor should they try to. Indeed, each prides itself on the unique bodies of papers and records on its shelves. Second, the system of arrangement and description of each repository is tailored both to suit the needs that the repository was created to serve and to handle the materials with which it works. Each repository faces a special situation with every new body of material to be arranged, described, and made available for use, since each must be processed on its own terms in order to preserve its integrity as a group.

Nor does the archival profession have the centralizing force of one institution that faces almost every problem likely to confront an archives. The National Archives, as important an institution as it has become, does not have the same relationship to the archival profession in the United States that the Library of Congress has with the library profession. It handles organizational records primarily, and can offer little guidance to those repositories that specialize in personal papers. Furthermore, its size, as well as the size of its various record groups, puts it in a class by itself: its problems and their solutions rarely are shared by the majority of repositories.

The archival profession has produced no person, either practioner or scholar, who has codified its ways or synthesized its knowledge to a degree equal to that achieved by Melvil Dewey for the library profession. The number of books and manuals that describe archival work and processes in general terms, rather than from the experience of a single institution, can be counted on one hand. Archivists have no equivalent to the *Anglo-American Cataloging Rules.*

Consequently, each institution establishes its own particular procedures suited to its special circumstances and holdings.

Records Don't Save Themselves

Archives do not exist at the mouth of a cornucopia, and records do not flow into a repository simply because it exists to receive them. To be effective in obtaining records, the archivist must play an active role in seeking material and in maintaining a channel for it to his repository. Within an organization, the archivist needs to fashion a records management system that controls and directs the records to the repository as through a pipeline. To work effectively the system must be, and be accepted as, a vital thread in the fabric of the organization it serves. In an institution collecting the archives of others for purposes of research, the successful archivist first determines what material is to be sought, then aggressively contacts the myriad of potential donors. Collecting emphasizes detective work to locate material and diplomacy to obtain it.

However effective the system, the wise archivist accessions no collections or record groups before they have been appraised for their permanent value. It is much easier to return materials brought in only for appraisal than to dispose of documents or entire collections formally accepted into the holdings. Accessioning acknowledges permanent value and signifies acceptance of the burdens and responsibilities of archival preservation.

Elements of both science and art characterize appraisal. Several specific considerations—among them quantity, age, and form of the material—bring objectivity to an appraisal decision. But only the artist's experience and intuition can determine the proper weight to be accorded any one of the factors, or the exact combination of them appropriate in a given situation.

Many archivists argue that appraisal is the most intellectual function of their profession. It requires both research to provide a context for understanding the creator's place in history, and the study and balancing of a host of specific factors concerning the records themselves. In assessing a body of records, the appraiser not only gauges value in terms of the research interests and business needs of today, but also must anticipate the demands of the patrons of tomorrow.

Material in an Archives Is There Forever But Not Entombed

Archivists seek and accept records for permanent preservation. This is a long-term commitment, and they do not make it lightly. Quite considerable resources—of staff time for processing; staff time for assisting patrons; costs of physical conservation, including proper housing and necessary restoration—are pledged when a body of material is accessioned for preservation in a future far beyond anyone's knowledge or imagination.

To reveal the full extent of the information in papers for which such a commitment has been made, days, weeks, often months are invested in sorting, arranging, and describing each body of material. Archivists believe it is better to take the time necessary to do this job thoroughly and properly than to cut corners and risk having information buried until uncovered by fortuitous accident. They perfect the arrangement and prepare at least the basic finding aids. As research interests change, new finding aids can be created. But the essential processing of the material should not need to be revised.

The commitment to permanent preservation, combined with the investment in processing, accounts for the archivist's abiding concern for security. "Security" in archival terms means prevention both of theft, mutilation, and other malicious acts recognizable under the law, and of disturbance of the order established during arrangement. Inadvertent misfiling or rearrangement of documents can eliminate information from use just as completely as theft.

To honor this covenant to permanent preservation, the archivist permits use of holdings only under supervision in the search room. Patrons are not allowed in the stacks. The holdings are not circulated. While every repository adopts certain rules to suit its particular situation, the standard provisions are included on the accompanying "Guide for Readers" employed in the Division of Special Collections at the University of Texas at Arlington.

Ranking close behind security among the archivist's chief concerns today is conservation. The term "conservation" can mean both measures anyone can take to slow deterioration of documents, and measures best left to a professional conservator. The steps taken to provide for the physical survival of each and every document become more important daily. Even the best paper deteriorates. Paper is made of organic materials. But the quality of paper in common use has declined steadily in inverse ratio to improvements in manufacturing. The archivist cannot stop the decay, only slow it through careful attention to the conditions under which paper is kept and regulation of the treatment it receives. Conservators say that providing proper conditions of housing and use is more important overall than any work they can do. Their work is slow and painstaking. It proceeds document by document, and simply cannot reach more than a small—the worst—part of the problem. Conservators also believe that no procedure should be done that cannot be undone. These are times of rapid development in the field of conservation. The usefulness of a new technique should not be denied a document by

GUIDE FOR READERS

DIVISION OF SPECIAL COLLECTIONS
UNIVERSITY OF TEXAS AT ARLINGTON

1. Leave briefcases, books, coats, etc., in the space provided.
2. **SMOKING** or other use of tobacco in any form **IS NOT PERMITTED** at any time.
3. Each reader is required to fill out the Reader's Application at the time of initial application. Positive identification is required of every reader. Such identification will be held by the staff until all items are returned in good condition
4. Use a pencil for all notes. Fountain pens, ball-point pens, or ink in any form **MAY NOT BE USED** in the reading room or conference room.
5. Fill out the call slip legibly and completely. **IT IS A PERMANENT RECORD.**
6. Ordinarily only one item (book, file folder, manuscript) may be used at a time. If the reader calls for more than one, others will be held at the desk and issued singly as required. Exceptions may be made at the discretion of the curator.
7. All materials must be used at a table in the reading room or the conference room. They will be brought to you by the staff, but you must return to the central desk. When the reader returns the item, it will be examined to determine that its condition is as good as when delivered to the reader.
8. Do not make marks of any kind in the material you use! Keep elbows and heavy objects off the books and manuscripts; never fold or otherwise disturb the physical state of the materials. The staff always welcomes information about cataloguing deficiencies, but under no circumstances shall the reader rearrange manuscript material or disturb the physical arrangement of individual manuscript pieces. If your work requires close examination of the stitching, paper, etc., consult the curator.
9. To obtain permission for any sort of photoduplication, to transcribe, to quote or publish from manuscript material, consult the curator.
10. Before leaving the reading room, the reader is required to secure a release slip from the attendant at the desk indicating that all materials issued you have been returned.
11. When photocopy, microfilm, or transcription of any manuscript or record group exists, it will be used by readers in lieu of the original. Only when close and careful textual examination is required will such originals be issued to qualified readers.
12. Please inquire in advance about the use of typewriters and tape recorders. In some cases, arrangements can be made for their use so long as other readers are not disturbed.
13. Group tours or class visits must be arranged well in advance to minimize the disturbance to readers.
14. A few reading glasses, markers, and book weights are available. Please ask for them when you need them.

short-sighted application of a procedure that, when something more effective becomes available, cannot be reversed. Conservators add, moreover, that experimentation by novices with little-understood conservation procedures risks permanent damage to documents. If a procedure fails, too often the damage done is irreparable and leaves the item in worse condition than before the work had begun.

Finally, understanding that permanent preservation means records are not thrown aside to make room for other records, archivists are always concerned about the adequacy of the storage space available to them. The number of collections and record groups under their care may grow at a relatively modest pace, considering the small percentage of records worthy of permanent preservation (3% to 5% in the average organization), nevertheless they continue accumulating ceaselessly.

Every Patron Is A Case

Archives (records) are for use, not dead storage. Indeed, use is inherent in the concept of permanent value, and archival preservation is accorded only to records expected to be used through the years.

The use made of an archives (institution), however, differs notably from that made of most libraries. The majority of patrons in any archives seek neither ready reference information, casual perusal of holdings, nor materials to take home for study at their leisure. They come to conduct research, usually of some depth and duration.

Beyond this, every person using an archives is unique. No two seek exactly the same information or go about their search in exactly the same way. Each has a special interest, a special viewpoint, and—because some information is necessary before one can know where to begin to look for information—a special knowledge of his subject. Since serendipity often plays a significant role in research, even two searchers who set out on the same path will follow different routes to the goal.

Moreover, the nature of archival practices and policies tends to magnify the individual nature of each researcher's quest. The random filing of collections and the individual arrangements within each, as contrasted with the simple subject/author order of books on library shelves, negates the concept of patrons searching in the stacks for pertinent sources. Hence the patron obtains archival material through finding aids and through the knowledge of the archivist. No finding aid could ever capture all the information on the holdings in the mind of the archivist who works with them every day. The archivist, moreover, not only assists the patron in using the finding aids, but continues to provide help by relating the researcher's specific topic to the records themselves. Actually, the searcher makes the fullest use of the resources in the archives by forming a team with the archivist.

As important as it is to serve each researcher who enters the archives, there is a greater need to be honored. The principle was put succinctly by the political leaders of colonial Maryland in 1650 when they permitted "the Records to be searched by any Inhabitant of this Province, Gratis, the party desiring such search being not impertinently troublesome." While the records are preserved for and are readily available to each person who comes to the archives, no person has the right to take that privilege from another. And it is the archivist's duty to see that the records are available for every researcher, not just the present one.

Archivists Ride the Horns of Dilemma

In the process of obtaining, preserving and making records available for research, archivists face several fundamental, interesting, and often irresolvable conflicts. Consequently, archivists must develop the ability to see both sides of each issue. They must appreciate, too, that their decisions will affect the present, the future, and ultimately, our knowledge of ourselves through our documentary heritage. The dilemmas occur throughout the archival field. The most common are sketched here in briefest outline.

Should the archivist be an "honest broker" or an activist in obtaining material? The collecting of material, even the existence of many archives, is heavily influenced by research trends and by the topics that attract each succeeding generation of researchers. Until recent times, research centered on traditional topics, such as politics, business, prominent figures, and wars. Records created by participants satisfied the demands of researchers.

Now it is different. Researchers have shifted their focus to include study of the masses heretofore undocumented. New technologies, like the tape recorder, make it possible to obtain information from persons who otherwise would be lost to history because they produced no paper records. The emphasis of society on statistics has brought many to the conclusion that saving only that material produced by those accustomed to creating records may not document our society evenly, which in turn will yield ill-balanced history. The question is put: Should the archivist help create the documents and information to be saved, or should he save only what reaches him through the sifter of time and circumstance? Within the organization the question becomes: Should the company archivist preside over those random files that come from thoughtful persons within the organization, or is his job to work to establish a system that feeds into the repository appropriate records from all areas of the business? Most archivists advocate the honest broker role in acquiring manuscripts and the systematic arrangement within the organization.

The archivist cannot keep everything, but strives to keep all that is possible and appropriate, and to do it systematically. Archivists are keenly aware that there is not space enough to save all records. But they know too that a document once discarded is gone forever. The only means of guarding against unnecessary destruction of documents, while protecting precious storage space from being filled with records of only temporary value, is systematic appraisal of records. Nevertheless, archivists constantly seek sufficient space to house pertinent records, driven by the knowledge that, in all fields and organizations, records of permanent value are being created every day.

Honoring both the Right to Know and the Right to Privacy places the archivist in a precarious position. This conflict is being fought throughout our society and is hardly unique to archives. It has come into archives and manuscript repositories as a by-product of the drive to acquire and use twentieth century material.

This dilemma traps the curator between his call to make material available to the researcher as quickly and fully as possible and his need to protect his ability to continue to receive valuable recent material. If donors feel the curator has violated, or may violate, their trust through premature release of sensitive data, or by not calling to their attention the existence of such data so that they could take steps to protect themselves, an entire collecting program could shrivel. Most archivists believe it to be more important to obtain material on condition it be closed temporarily than to lose a collection altogether by insisting on a release date unacceptable to the donor.

Technology is part of the solution and part of the problem. The capacity to make photographic duplicates of documents and collections saves a researcher's time, but it is no general balm for the archivist.

Brittle papers, large books, and tightly bound volumes of every size are tyrannized by the photocopy machine. Its design aggravates rather than eases the strains, for it requires the items to be flattened mercilessly on the cold platen of the machine.

Microfilm is neither a panacea nor an inexpensive alternative to preservation of most original documents. It serves well: 1) in providing duplicate copies of materials needed in more than one office, 2) in making possible the circulation of documents, the originals of which are not allowed out of the search room, 3) in providing a security copy, and 4) in reducing the handling of frequently consulted records. But the amount of work required to prepare a body of records for filming (which includes all steps normally taken in arranging and describing the records, plus the additional chores of preparing descriptive material necessary specifically for the microfilming) cause archivists with small staffs to think twice. Once material is on film, the archivist confronts a new set of concerns. Two copies, not one, are necessary of any film. One is used, the other—the master negative—is saved strictly for reproduction. Film is easily damaged passing through a reader; in time it will become illegible and need to be replaced, and thus will be an ongoing expense. (As yet, microfiche has not become popular in archival reading rooms.) Film is more susceptible to damage by fire and atmospheric conditions than is paper.

Use justifies preservation, but preservation may have to prescribe use. The archivist is charged to make documents as readily and fully available for use as possible. Yet he also must protect them from damage in use, even from excessive wear and tear resulting from routine consultation. By preventing circulation of materials, requiring use of pencils instead of pens, and prohibiting food and drink in the search room, the one concern is served without compromising the other. In some instances, photocopying must be prohibited. In more extreme cases, documents may have to be retired from general use and brought out only in special circumstances. The archivist cannot watch a document being destroyed by use, so that the present patron has the benefit of it but future generations do not.

The purpose of archives is strongly endorsed, but archival budgets rarely, rarely provide adequate resources. Society recognizes the importance of records. Governments, businesses, even our own personal lives run on paper records. Few doubt the importance of maintaining certain records no longer used in the daily course of events. As individuals and families we religiously store these in cardboard boxes. Governments maintain agencies to care for them.

Yet proper archival preservation of records is work that requires substantial human labor, not just a dark corner. And humans will not soon, if ever, be replaced by machines. Thus the cost of archival work can be substantial. Since records seemingly always can sit in a box a little longer, other expenditures often claim precedence.

Statistics from the use of archival holdings rarely help substantially to justify an appropriate budget. One person consulting part of one collection, or even several collections, for a day, a week, or a month compiles nowhere near the statistics for an annual report, compared with those of the average circulation desk. Leaving an archival program in limbo can compromise an organization, however, by depriving it of information when data is needed. The value of documents that sustain a position in a legal proceeding cannot be measured by or equated to a statistic for the number of times records are consulted. Similarly, in historical, humanities and social science research, the primary sources—particularly contemporary records—are the heart of a work; secondary, printed references provide flesh for the bones.

Hence archivists work incessantly on increasing public awareness, understanding and appreciation of both their holdings and their work.

Should the archivist be scholar or businessman? In this age of inflation and cost accounting, more and more archivists believe that the survival of their repositories depends upon translating their work into dollars and cents by which superiors can appreciate their contribution. The result is a devaluation of the importance of scholarship as an attribute of an archivist. Instead, mastery of techniques increasingly becomes the dominant trait. But to serve the researcher fully, the archivist needs a sound foundation in the subject fields, represented by users of the holdings. Business acumen and scholarly aptitude both are needed, simply in different contexts.

The Process

Almost all materials in an archives pass down a similar road. First they come to the repository through a system of records management or the work of collecting. Second, either before or after arrival, they are appraised. Once the archivist is convinced that the files have historical value, the materials are accessioned, processed (arranged and described), housed, and made available to patrons for reference. If the papers are in poor physical condition, they can be treated in a conservation laboratory.

Acquisition

System is essential if the archives of an organization is to receive the records that belong there. Too many institutions lose the value of their records by permitting officers to treat the files as personal property. In fact, these files are the corporate memory, without which the organization risks repeating product failures, being unable to substantiate positions in legal cases, and losing the pride rooted in the organization's achievements and documented in a good company history. Records management is the system to which increasing numbers of organizations are turning.

Records management grew out of archival work. The unprecedented volume and the contemporaneity of records coming to government archives during World War II demanded that records keepers develop a means for controlling records prior to their accessioning into an archives. The techniques of records management are framed to assure the efficient and economical recording of information, to improve access to information in the office, and to see that records no longer useful to an office do not clog its information-keeping operation. In practical terms, records managers design both forms and filing systems, in order to speed retrieval of information and to assure that records, as the number of times they are consulted drops, are removed from office filing cabinets. Archivists refine the system by segregating records of permanent value to insure their preservation. Consulting with office personnel, records managers "schedule" records, that is, determine that period during which the records are needed in the office for regular use. After this term, which may range from several months to a year or two, they are retired to a records center for another period specified on the schedule. Records centers basically are warehouses for records where files still consulted from time to time for office business, and files needed to satisfy legal or financial requirements can be kept at less cost than in an office. At the conclusion of the second period on the schedule, the records are disposed of—either placed in the archives or destroyed. As a general rule only 3% to 5% of modern organizational records end up in an archives.

Obtaining records through a managed system requires a familiarity with the use records receive in each office, and with the organization's history and structure. Collecting papers from outside an organization for research emphasizes instead conversance in three other fields. One is the subject area in which collecting will be done. Primarily this knowledge permits the archivist to determine which materials have value for the subject field. But as the staff prepares finding aids, it also fosters balanced descriptions. Second, knowledge of the availability of material to be collected is essential. The archivist must locate desired material through recommendations of former donors, newspaper stories, and intuition. In addition, the archivist should determine whether another archives is already collecting similar bodies of materials and building an identical research collection. Duplication of effort both squanders institutional resources and forces researchers to visit ever more archives, thus compromising the chances of their seeing all of the pertinent documentation on their subject. Third, even if no other archives has been collecting in the field, the archivist should inquire as to whether enough researchers are interested in using the material to justify the work of collecting.

Appraisal

Whatever the route of records and papers to the archivist's door, they are admitted only after appraisal of their historical value. (Archivists distinguish "appraisal" from "evaluation," which to them means establishing monetary worth.) No one ever has, or ever will, develop a foolproof yardstick for determining enduring value. Nevertheless, in selecting records for permanent preservation, all archivists recognize that what they are preserving primarily is information. They know that they cannot save every scrap of paper, yet they try to save as much as is warranted and possible. Fortunately, the factors that count in the archivist's scale of historical value are similar whether applied to archival records or historical manuscripts collections. Eight principal factors are considered. They are not, and could not be, listed in priority order, for the weight given each varies with every body of material appraised.

Age The turn of the twentieth century forms a watershed for the appraisal of records by their age. The older a pre-twentieth-century document, the more likely the archivist will save it, simply because the farther back one goes in time the less writing was done and has survived. Scarcity is a principal ingredient in weighing material on the scale of age. For large series of the twentieth-century, such as case files composed of similar information about many persons, the problem is documenting the group while reducing the bulk. Some archivists trust random sampling. Others want to use random sampling and, in addition, select certain records for preservation. Still others doubt the value of sampling at all.

Volume Normally, the larger the quantity, the more selective the archivist must be. However, groups of documents that show action over time are generally more prized than lone items.

Form Few archives can afford to store duplicates, either exact copies or extensive repetitive files, such as financial records containing both books of daily entry and books in which this data is cumulated. Similarly, certain types of material—correspondence and diaries/minutes to name two—normally carry information more frequently used by researchers than do others. These are sought more diligently, and in case of doubt will more likely be saved.

Evidential Characteristics The archivist reviews the group for the evidence it reveals of the functioning of the creator and will be prone to save records documenting the organization, policy, functions, decisions, and performance of the creator.

Informational Characteristics Records are assessed on the basis of the information they contain on persons, places, events and actions other than those having strictly evidential value. Sometimes simply the degree to which the useful information is concentrated or disbursed through a sizeable series will affect the decision to retain a large body of records.

Administrative Value Historical value is not always exclusive. Within an organization the archives may receive records, such as minutes or personnel data, that must be kept not only for historical value, but also for its continuing financial, legal, or administrative value.

Research Values Under this umbrella, the archivist considers several values. One is the completeness of the documentation in a collection. All archivists know that the whole has a value greater than the sum of the parts. In other words, because all aspects of a matter can be seen in a body containing all the documentation originally produced on the matter, an archivist likely will retain the documents of lesser value because they are within the collection. If only the lesser documents—for example, financial records alone—had survived, it is unlikely that they would be kept. A second value is the intelligibility of documents. Doodlings, even if produced by a prominent person, are useless. Similarly, illegible documents are worthless, unless advances in technology someday make it possible to retrieve faded writing. A third value is the uniqueness of the material. The archivist considers the appropriateness of keeping documents duplicated not only in the holdings of his own repository, but also among the files of another repository.

Repository Collecting Policy Each repository should establish a clear policy outlining the subject areas from which it will seek and accept material. No institution can accept every body of material offered. Thus records of acknowledged value by all measures may not be accessioned into a repository because they fall outside its collecting sphere.

Accessioning

Satisfied of the historical value of a body of papers or records, the archivist formally accepts the material into the repository by accessioning it. In an accession book he notes the title of the materials obtained, the date received, the nature of the receipt, whether a gift, purchase or loan (precious little is accepted on loan any more), and conditions, if any, attached to the material. All documents preceding and arising out of the transaction are accumulated in a separate accession file.

Many repositories conclude the accessioning process by preparing a form, like the one reproduced on the following page, with which they can easily control the work of arrangement and description to follow.

Arrangement

The work of arrangement often begins when archivists learn that a body of papers or records is coming to the repository. Archivists want the order existing at that moment to be the order of the material when it reaches the archives. They are not bound to retain this arrangement forever simply because it exists, but they do not want to lose that opportunity through neglect. Consequently, when they can, archivists offer to pack collections for transport. By so doing, the order is preserved as the material goes into boxes. Equally important, an accurate inventory insures that the order is not inadvertently scrambled later as the material comes out.

Despite the archivist's best efforts, many collections seem to arrive fresh from a giant combine that takes the papers, jumbles them, and then bales them in old suitcases, steamer trunks, and cardboard boxes. If a prior accession of the same group has been received, then the new material may be arranged in conformity with it. Otherwise, the archivist must create order. Therein lies one of the great challenges of archival work, for an order must be found that clearly and honestly reveals the nature, quality and extent of the information in the collection or record group.

The creating of order is more the work of the curator of a historical manuscripts repository than of the archivist in an archives. But the tools employed by the curator in both arrangement and description are the same as those the archivist uses, particularly in describing the records on his shelves.

Curators often begin creating order by focusing on the types of material in the collection. Since anyone can tell one type from another, it is easy to begin mentally sorting scrambled papers from a steamer trunk using this tool. But on a broader plane, patrons find an arrangement by types contributes to their ability to assess the value of a body of papers for research. They know, for example, that correspondence, diaries, and minutes normally contain more substantive information valuable to them than do other types, such as financial records.

Accession   Permanent   Accession
Number _____ Location _____ Date _____

ARCHIVES
GEORGIA STATE UNIVERSITY

<u>ACCESSION RECORD</u>

Name of Collection:

Quantity and Description:

Source: Restrictions:

Processing Record
(Enter your initials and the date you complete a step)

PROCESSING	STEPS	TYPING
	1. Work-to-do card	
_____	2. Inventory	_____
_____	3. Housing	
_____	4. Labels	_____
_____	5. Descriptive Catalog Sheet	_____
_____	6. News release	_____
_____	7. Processed archival and Library material filed separately	
	8. Card files:	
	a. Collections cards	_____
	b. Chronological file	_____
	c. Printed collections	_____
_____	d. Index	_____
	9. NUCMC	_____

In actually arranging any body of material, elements of both horizontal and vertical order are used. On the document level, for example, the individual items may be placed chronologically, alphabetically, or in a combination of both. Letters could be arranged alphabetically by author and then, where there is more than one letter by a single author, chronologically. The detailed work of arrangement, insuring a perfect alphabet or chronology, occurs, of course, at the document level. In particularly large bodies of material and in repositories with voluminous holdings, time often simply does not exist for such close attention to order.

File units today consist most commonly of single items grouped into folders. Usually the original order of the folders, if preserved, will be chronological, alphabetical, or by types of material. If the order has been lost, the archivist normally finds one of these three a suitable framework for establishing a system. In either case, each file unit should be an exclusive entity housing all the documents within whatever grouping of papers the file unit represents.

Arrangement on both the document and file unit levels actually perfects the order at the series level. The goal of preservation of the original order is pursued most rigorously on the series level. The decision of the creator to file information one way or another not only governs how a person, present or future, finds the information, but can also tell much about the nature and efficiency of the creator of the files. Equally basic, the official character of files is rooted at this level. Destroy the original order here and only the information in the documents remains, forever widowed by loss of the perspective of the creator's construction of the files.

Curators unite with archivists in recognizing the importance of ascertaining the original order before determining an arrangement for a body of documents; especially before physically altering the location of any document. They are, on the other hand, less hesitant than archivists about revising an order that poorly reveals the information within the group. Archivists have to be concerned about the continuity of the organization of which they and the records under their care are a part. Curators deal largely with separate and independent units, continuity rarely stretching beyond the single body of papers.

On the series level, as on those levels beneath it, whether or not the original order survives, archivist and curator alike frame exclusive categories to insure that like documents are located in similar places. As much as possible, series should follow but one system—chronology, topics, or types of material.

Normally, however, the systems of arrangement followed on the series, file unit, and document levels are different from each other. As a result, every document or item of information can be located in more than one way.

Through the series level, archivists conceive of the levels of arrangement as building blocks in a pyramid of arrangement and description. Each entry on each higher level of arrangement summarizes all the entries on the levels immediately beneath it. Thus carbon copies of letters dated in 1910 might make up one file unit of "letters sent, 1910," while several file units-worth of letters received could combine into the subseries "letters received, 1910." Those two groupings would then combine into the series "correspondence, 1910." (Correspondence by definition means letters received and letters sent—both sides of a communication.) The series of correspondence in turn combines with other series—financial records and diaries—to form the record group or collection. Consider the hypothetical Smith Family Papers.

Smith Family Papers, 1910–1914 (collection)

Correspondence, 1910	(series)
Letters sent, 1910	(subseries and file unit)
Letters received, 1910	(subseries)
Jones, Jan.–Oct.	(file unit, with documents ordered by date)
Mason, March	(file unit, with documents ordered by date)
Williams, June–Aug.	(file unit, with documents ordered by date)
Financial Records, 1913–1914	(series)
Day Books, 1913	(subseries)
Jan.–June	(file unit—one book)
July–Dec.	(file unit)
Bills and receipts, 1914 and undated	(subseries)
Feb.	(file unit)
Oct.	(file unit)
Undated	(file unit)
Diary, 1912	(series)

The record group or collection is the basic organizational unit out of which the series and file units flow. It is essential to the system as the framework within which arrangement occurs on the subordinate levels. It is the unit to which the principle of respect des fonds applies. Nevertheless, little arrangement occurs on this level. In the administration of a repository, the record group/collection is fundamental as a basic unit of measure for recording statistics of accessions, use and holdings.

Convenience governs order on the repository level. Record groups and collections are arranged to avoid having to shift large quantities of paper as new material is added to the shelves. While categories of collections may be separated in the stacks by broad date periods or subjects, and while archives are segregated from manuscript collections, both normally are shelved in the order work on them is completed. Frequently, however, the most heavily used bodies of material will be located near the research room to reduce time in retrieval.

After a collection/record group has been received into a repository, it is worked three times. First the archivist goes through it, without rearranging anything, learning about the material. He wants to determine the original arrangement and condition of the accession, as well as contextual information on the provenance and creator. With this information, the archivist should be able to conclude rather precisely the order in which to place the material, whether to leave it entirely as received, or to revamp the arrangement completely.

Second, the material is sorted accordingly. If it is in a good, usable order, the archivist begins working from the series level down, simply confirming and perfecting the system already established. In the case of disarranged collections that require substantial or total reordering, work begins at the document level and proceeds upward. In either case, the archivist studies the physical condition of the papers to determine whether special conservation or restoration treatment is necessary. In addition, oversize material—anything too large, when unfolded or unrolled, to fit in the box with the main body of material—is removed to receive special housing. Documents kept folded will in time split at the seams, and thereby create more expense in restoration than the cost of space to store them flat. Finally, non-paper records and special forms of paper records—including recording tape, film, microforms, material in machine readable form, maps, photographs, and certain printed material—are also removed for special housing and attention.

Third, the archivist reassembles the collection, placing the material in folders and boxes as appropriate, and preparing necessary labels.

Description

Four elements make up a well-rounded program of description. 1) Inventories describe collections and record groups individually. 2) Indices and lists prepared for consultation within the repository, and 3) a guide published for use externally, treat the holdings of one repository. Finally, 4) national cumulations of information offer capsule data both on individual bodies of material and on repositories.

Inventories describe bodies of papers and records by the subseries and series that compose them. These documents can take several forms, but always reveal the specific arrangement of the material. They include data on the quantity, dates, and types of material in the collection as a whole, as well as in the individual series. In manuscripts repositories a box listing is common and a folder listing is not unusual. Both are rare in archives of large organizations. Of course the archives have the information, but simply lack the time to prepare such close descriptions for the formal inventory. Basically, this list is a detailed table of contents.

A "Scope and Content Note" summarizes in a paragraph or page the contents of the entire collection. Here the archivist presents a narrative assessment of the richness or shallowness of the information in the collection, without reference necessarily to the arrangement of the records, though full, large, or otherwise notable series may be singled out.

Placing the collection in the perspective of its provenance, inventories should contain a sketch biography or history, as appropriate, of the creator. Normally, the sketch will repeat little information in the scope and content note, for rarely does a body of material cover fully all facets of a person's life or exactly mirror the work of an organization. Commonly, individuals and organizations gather information on matters of interest. This collected data could well form a series or subseries, and yet the activity of collecting it might not be important enough to deserve a mention in the history or biography.

Large repositories often produce more than one inventory for each record group and sizeable collection. A preliminary inventory helps the archivist to gain control (learn about and record his knowledge) of a body of material, especially in those cases in which it is likely that additional files will be added. Later, after the collection or record group is complete—"closed" in the archivist's vocabulary—and the repository has finished a careful, thorough arrangement and description of the material, a regular inventory (often called just "an inventory") is produced. The difference between it and the preliminary inventory is simply that the information in the regular inventory is more complete and accurate. Small closed collections can usually be processed adequately in one operation, eliminating the need for a preliminary inventory.

Each inventory describes a single body of records or papers. But topics of research often require information drawn from many collections and record groups. Hence, archivists develop annotated lists of collections and groups containing information on frequently asked-for topics. Curators do likewise, but, more than archivists, might also create indices (usually mistitled "card catalogs" because they are maintained on cards). Some curators index the inventories; others, with more time and smaller holdings, index directly from the documents. Many curators used to index to the document level so thoroughly that, in essence, the item was "cataloged." But time and quantity no longer permit this luxury. Archivists do not mourn the loss, because the practice violates the archivist's cardinal rule to deal with material in groups. The indices to all the collections are intermingled in one central subject index. For a chronological index, specific periods are established and cards inserted for each body of papers containing documents dated during any period. With these cards, a person studying the Great Depression, for example, could readily locate records likely to be pertinent merely by looking at entries for the decade of the 1930s. Some archives maintain similar indices for geographical regions, others for autographs, still others for types of material, as diaries.

In producing a guide describing each body of material in a repository, the archivist draws information from inventories, particularly from the scope and content notes. Subject content, not arrangement, is the heart of this publication designed to inform potential users distant from the repository of its holdings. Many archivists find a guide project useful for the index that results from the work and for the review of holdings it requires.

National accumulations of data give the archivist another means of broadcasting information on his holdings. Through these a researcher can often learn not only of the existence of a repository, but also of specific collections and groups of interest. The *National Union Catalog of Manuscript Collections,* compiled and issued by the Library of Congress, publishes descriptions of individual collections in a unit-card format. It specifically excludes records of an institution held by that institution. Journals in several fields carry reports of records and papers recently received and/or opened for research. Finally, the *Directory of Archives and Manuscript Repositories in the United States,* published by the National Historical Publications and Records Commission, not only lists repositories by city and state, but also provides succinct summary of the holdings of each.

Conservation

One's initial encounter with the field of conservation is often sobering. A person first learns that deterioration cannot be stopped, only slowed, and then finds that the field seems governed by more "do nots" than "dos." Nevertheless, an archivist, no matter how unschooled in chemistry, can contribute significantly to the preservation of the material under his care.

No conservation measures are more helpful than those simple, precautionary ones each archivist can take with regard to:

Light—Expose documents to light no longer than necessary, especially the ultraviolet rays of the sun and flourescent bulbs. Ultraviolet rays accelerate the chemical processes of degradation.

Atmosphere—For paper records, maintain an average temperature of 68 degrees Farenheit and a relative humidity near 60 percent to combat brittleness on the one hand and mold and mildew on the other. Photographs survive better in a cooler and drier atmosphere—no higher than 60 degrees Farenheit—and near 40 percent relative humidity. If these ideals cannot be achieved exactly, a constant environment is preferable to one frequently changing. Finally, an atmosphere limited in dust and fumes is preferred, if appropriate filters can be installed on air handling equipment.

Infestation—Fumigating materials before bringing them into the repository and prohibiting food and drink during their use remove a source of, and encouragement to, vermin and rodents.

Housing—Unfold and house documents flat to avoid placing stress on creases. Archival boxes and records-center cartons designed for records storage are far preferable to filing cabinets for safe, long-term storage. The use of *acid-free* folders helps to preserve documents by not aggravating the problem of internal decay. The acid used in the manufacture of paper, if not removed (which it hardly is in cheaper papers), becomes a leading contributor to deterioration. Avoiding the use of folders high in acid content protects documents from a source of additional, harmful acid.

CORRESPONDENCE, 1845-1927

Letters Sent, 1845-1911

Main Series of the Superintendent

1. **LETTERS SENT. Aug. 1845-Nov. 1865. 11 vols. (Nos. 2, 4-6, 8, 10, 11, 18, and 20-22). 2 ft.**

Arranged chronologically. A name index is in volume 5. Partial name and subject indexes are in volumes 11 and 18 while a complete name and subject index is in volume 21.

Fair copies of letters sent by the Superintendent to public and private individuals and businesses, including the Secretary of the Navy, applicants to the Academy, midshipmen, instructors, and merchants. Included also are letters to the Bureau of Ordnance and Hydrography.

In volume 2 are letters sent by Comdr. Franklin Buchanan relating to plans for the establishment of the school and rules for the selection of midshipmen and their training. Letters sent relating to the summer practice cruises of the U.S.S. *Preble,* commanded by Lt. Thomas T. Craven, June-September 1852, which established sea duty as training for midshipmen, are in volume 4.

Letters sent by the Superintendent to the Secretary of the Navy and to Navy Department bureaus for the period October 1864-November 1865 are not copied in this entry but are copied in entries 8, 9, and 12. For press copies of letters sent, October 1865-December 1911, see entry 3. Letters in this entry and in entry 4 relate to cruises for the midshipmen.

The letters in this entry have been reproduced as NARS Microfilm Publication M945, *Letters Sent by the Superintendent of the U.S. Naval Academy, 1845-65.*

2. **REGISTERS TO PARTS OF ENTRIES 3, 9, 12, 16, 22, AND 23, AND ENTRY 29. 1888-1906. 20 vols. (Nos. 286-305). 5 ft.**

Arranged by year, thereunder alphabetically by initial letter or first two letters of surname or subject, thereunder by sent and received, and thereunder by month and day.

Each volume registers both letters sent and received, with the exception of the volumes for 1901 and 1903-6, in which only letters received are registered. The information given for letters sent includes name or title of addressee, subject, a summary of the letter's contents, location or book and page numbers of the letter sent, date of the letter, and file and record number assigned to any letter received on the same subject. Few entries are found in the "action" column, and in the 1902 volume the heading "action" was replaced by bureau number under which the file numbers of all incoming bureau letters were entered.

The information for letters received is generally the same as that for letters sent. In some instances the subject of the letter has been substituted for the name of the sender. The file and record number is that of the letter received in entry 29, and the book and page numbers refer to the location of the letter sent in reply. Book and page numbers have been omitted in the registers of letters received, 1902-6. Numbers assigned by Navy Department bureaus to letters sent to the Academy ("Bureau or Letter Nos.") have been entered in the registers for 1900 and 1902-6.

Numbers presently assigned to volumes in this record group were not in use at the time these registers were prepared; therefore the volume numbers referred to in the registers are the numbers appearing on the volumes at that time. The table in appendix A lists the present volume number, the corresponding volume numbers used in the register, and the entry in this inventory in which the volume can be found.

Letters sent registered in this entry can be found in the volumes, as indicated in appendix A, of the following:

Entry 3: press copy volumes 102, 103, 105-122, 129, 133, 139, 179, and 180

Entry 9: press copy volumes 86 and 104

Entry 12: press copy volumes 124, 125, 128, 130-132, 134, 140, 161, 162, and 165-167

Entry 16: press copy volumes 61 and 96

Entry 22: press copy volumes 93, 94, 98, 137, 138, 126, 127, 141, 142, 144, and 145

Entry 23: part of press copy volume 90

3. **PRESS COPIES OF LETTERS SENT. Oct. 1865-Dec. 1911. 96 vols. (Nos. 31-44, 71-76, 78, 80-82, 95, 102, 103, 105-122, 129, 133, 139, 178-191, 191A, and 192-224). 11 ft.**

Arranged chronologically. Name indexes are in volumes 31-35, 38-44, 71-76, 78, 80, 82, and 95. Name and subject indexes are in volumes 31, 36, 37,

---

Page from *Inventory of the Records of the United States Naval Academy* (Washington: National Archives and Records Service, 1975).

SERIES

Page from *Register of Robert J. Dana Papers* (Pullman, Washington: Washington State University, 1974).

Scope and Content Note

The Blackwell family papers trace the evolution of woman's rights in many fields—political, religious, medical, economic, and domestic. Beginning with the pioneer work of Lucy Stone, who in 1847 gave her first lecture on woman's rights, and continuing to 1950, the year of the death of her daughter, Alice Stone Blackwell, the papers present a century of dramatic change in the status of women, with total victory for many of the causes these women and others in their family espoused.

Of the 20 family members represented by groups of papers in this collection, those having the most papers are Alice Stone Blackwell, Elizabeth Blackwell, Henry Brown Blackwell, Kitty Barry Blackwell, and Lucy Stone (Mrs. Henry B. Blackwell).

Elizabeth Blackwell was the first woman to receive an M.D. degree, and her extensive diaries (1836–1908), family and general correspondence, and speeches and writings document her struggle to open the medical profession to women in the United States. Included in her correspondence are numerous letters from Lady Byron and Florence Nightingale, who gave support to her medical work abroad. Dr. Blackwell wrote widely on various aspects of medicine, and her papers include many of her published works which are unavailable elsewhere.

In 1854 Dr. Blackwell adopted a 6-year-old orphan, Kitty Barry,[1] who lived with her throughout her life. After Dr. Blackwell's return to England in 1869, Kitty Barry became her secretary, companion, and nurse as well as her daughter. There is a large group of Kitty Barry's correspondence which sheds considerable light on Dr. Blackwell's years in England, and the letters she received from Alice Stone Blackwell report on the careers of the various Blackwells in the United States. In 1921 Kitty Barry Blackwell left England and spent her remaining years with Alice Stone Blackwell.

The papers of Lucy Stone, a leading antislavery and woman's rights advocate, include correspondence with Susan B. Anthony, Henry Ward Beecher, William Lloyd Garrison, Sarah Grimké, Julia Ward Howe, Lydia Mott, Wendell Phillips, and Elizabeth Cady Stanton. Her papers include many of her speeches and articles, and among her biographical papers are important reminiscences recorded by her husband, Henry B. Blackwell, and her daughter, Alice Stone Blackwell.

---

[1] From the papers, it appears that she was known as Kitty Barry during Elizabeth Blackwell's lifetime, and Kitty Barry Blackwell after Dr. Blackwell's death. Her given name is spelled alternately Katharine and Katherine.

Page from *Register of the Blackwell Family, Carrie Chapman Catt, and the National American Woman Suffrage Association Papers* (Washington: Library of Congress, 1975).

Folding and moisture have taken their toll
on this 175-year-old document.

Handling of Materials—Prohibit the use of ink near documents, as well as both tracing and marking directly on them. Pressure sensitive tape, and especially rubber cement and rubber bands, can leave indelible stains on documents and are not a permanent means of holding papers together. Archivists never use them on permanently valuable materials.

The list can go on. But the point of all these actions is to take every precaution—especially common sense, inexpensive ones—to prolong the life of the irreplaceable documents.

Trained conservators should be consulted for the treatment of items in poor condition. The most common treatment in former years was lamination. In this process, using a Barrow laminator, heat and pressure fuse acetate and tissue with the document to give it strength and protection. However, lamination is not used as universally as it once was in the United States because of the detrimental effects of the heat and the work of reversing the process if that becomes necessary. Many conservation laboratories now prefer the encapsulation process. In encapsulation, a document is sandwiched between two sheets of polyester film and sealed in place. The procedure uses no heat or pressure, and is readily reversible. The glare, weight, and bulk of the polyester, however, keep archivists searching for improvements in the technique.

Regardless of which process is used, each document is treated beforehand to remove the acidity in it and to introduce a buffer against the return of the acid condition. Deacidification usually involves impregnating the paper with a solution. It is done only after careful testing of the document to be certain that the ink or other medium of writing will not run or fade during the treatment.

The work of a conservation laboratory is not cheap. But compared to the loss of a prized document, it is a bargain. The names and locations of commercial laboratories in the United States can be obtained from the American Institute for Conservation of Historic and Artistic Works, 1522 K Street, N.W., Suite 804, Washington, D.C. 20005.

Reference

Each person who comes to an archives to do research is registered, both as a security measure and so that the archivist can contact the patron in the future if the need arises. The archivist then interviews the patron to learn the nature and topic of his research, to determine what kind of assistance the person needs, and to explain the regulations and other considerations affecting use of the repository.

By understanding the approach of each patron the archivist can lead him to both the obvious and the not-so-obvious sources. Each may consult the same record, but reach it in a different manner and glean from it different information. Genealogists—the largest single group using the nation's archives today—seek quite specific data on individuals. They search by names, geography, and types of materials (census records, tax lists, wills and probate records). Academic researchers commonly study trends and work to elaborate concepts. Names, geography, and periods of history are avenues to their broader, more elusive topics. Finally, employees using old office files normally search by reference to a filing system familiar to them.

The archivist analyzes each patron as a researcher, for different persons need different kinds and amounts of assistance. The job of the reference archivist is to help patrons carry out their research, not to do it for them. The archivist gives information about the records: the nature of their contents, their arrangement, their provenance, tailoring the information to suit the needs of the researcher. The researcher must study for himself the information in the records. Only the archivist within an organization is apt to perform lengthy searches, and then strictly for others inside the organization. Research repositories usually maintain a list of persons willing to do research for a fee.

The archivist who serves the researcher best, especially in a manuscript repository, commands two areas of knowledge. Archives—the system of arrangement and description used in the repository, as well as the records likely to be pertinent to the researcher's subject—is the more important. But the greater the archivist's acquaintance with the fields of study represented by the bulk of researchers using the repository, the better job he can do of relating the subjects being researched to the records as they are maintained on the shelves.

Every request to use material in the search room must be submitted on a form. After use in pulling the desired material and compiling statistics, the forms are kept for several years in case a theft is discovered. The forms can reveal the materials a given person used or the persons who had access to a given body of materials.

An essential facet of reference activity is insuring the integrity and safe handling of the material serviced to a patron. Search rooms are designed to provide stations for at least one staff member, preferably more, in the room. The staff assists and, equally important, watches the patrons. Patron consciousness that staff is present is the archivist's most certain defense against inadvertent misfiling of items by a patron or outright attempts at theft. To further discourage attempts at theft, the archivist restricts the personal belongings a patron can take to the research table. When the patron leaves, personal belongings and papers are searched. Those archivists whose repositories have been victimized advocate a prearranged plan for dealing with the emergency of theft, so that all staff members know how to react.

Most archives include with their rules and regulations, a copy of which is provided to each patron, a suggested form for citing material in the repository. This assists a novice unfamiliar with the technique of proper citation. The archivist hopes it will cause the researcher who publishes to include adequate information in citations, so that sources referred to by one person can be found by another. At a minimum, this information includes, in reverse order, the name of the repository, the title of the collection/record group, the series or place in the collection where the document(s) is located, and a description of the item(s) cited:

> Bill Jones to John Doe, February 9, 1891, deed [information on the document], Legal Records [series], Robert Smith Papers [collection], West University Archives [repository].

Reference easily can become the tail that wags the archival dog. Patrons in the search room deserve service, even if it means pulling workers from processing to assist the search room staff. But pulling staff from preparing material for reference hampers equally essential processing work. Consequently, archivists try to maintain the pace of processing while serving every research request. By so doing, they strive both to meet the demands of the present and to prepare to satisfy those of the future.

Suggestions for Further Reading

Barrow, William J. *Manuscripts and Documents: Their Deterioration and Restoration.* 2d. ed.: Charlottesville, 1972.

Berner, Richard C. "Manuscript Catalogs and Other Finding Aids: What Are Their Relationships?" *American Archivist* 34 (Oct 1971): 367–372.

Bordin, Ruth B., and Robert M. Warner. *The Modern Manuscript Library.* New York, 1966.

Brichford, Maynard J. *Archives and Manuscripts: Appraisal and Accessioning.* Chicago, 1977.

Brooks, Philip C. *Research in Archives, The Use of Unpublished Primary Sources.* Chicago, 1969.

Burke, Frank G. "The Impact of the Specialist on Archives." *College and Research Libraries* 33 (July 1972): 312–317.

Casterline, Gail Farr. *Archives and Manuscripts: Exhibits.* Chicago, 1980.

Christian, John F. and Shonnie Finnegan. "On Planning an Archives." *American Archivist* 37 (Oct 1974): 573–578.

Cunha, George M. *Conservation of Library Materials.* 2d. ed.: Metuchen, 1971.

Densmore, Christopher. "Understanding and Using Early Nineteenth Century Account Books," *Midwestern Archivist* V (1980): 5–20.

Duckett, Kenneth. *Modern Manuscripts: A Practical Manual for Their Management, Care, and Use.* Nashville, 1975.

Dunn, Walter S., Jr. *Cataloging Ephemera: A Procedure for Small Libraries.* American Association for State and Local History Technical Leaflet no.58.

Euper, Sister Jo Ann. "Starting A Religious Congregation Archives: Administrative Formulas for Better or Worse." *Midwestern Archivist* V (1980): 21–28.

Gordon, Robert S. "Suggestions for Organization and Description of Archival Holdings of Local Historical Societies." *American Archivist* 26 (Jan 1963): 19–39.

Gracy, David B., II. *Archives and Manuscripts: Arrangement and Description.* Chicago, 1977.
_____. "Establishing an Archives." *Georgia Archive* I (Fall, 1972): 20–29.

Heinrich, Dorothy L. "Establishing an Ethnic Collection in a Small Institution." *Midwestern Archivist* II (1977): 41–48.

Holbert, Sue E. *Archives and Manuscripts: Reference and Access.* Chicago, 1977.

Kemp, Edward C. *Manuscript Solicitation for Libraries, Special Collections, Museums and Archives.* Littleton, 1978.

Lathrop, Alan K. "The Archivist and Architectural Records." *Georgia Archive* V (Sum 1977): 25–32.

Leisinger, Albert H. Jr. *Microphotography for Archives.* Washington, 1968.

Lytle, Richard H., ed. *Management of Archives and Manuscript Collections for Librarians.* Special issue of *Drexel Library Quarterly* 11, Jan 1975.

Maedke, Wilmer O. Mary F. Robek, Gerald F. Brown, *Information and Records Management.* Beverly Hills, 1974.

Ricks, Artel. "Records Management as an Archival Function." *Records Management Quarterly* 11 no. 2 (Apr 1977): 12–18, 20.

Schellenberg, Theodore R. *The Management of Archives.* New York, 1965.

Smith, Charles. *Micrographics Handbook.* Dedham, Mass., 1978.

Society of American Archivists. *College and University Archives: Selected Readings.* Chicago, 1979.

Stewart, Virginia. "A Primer on Manuscript Field Work." *Midwestern Archivist* I, no. 2 (1976): 3–20.

"Problems of Confidentiality in the Administration of Personal Cases Records" *American Archivist* 37 (Jul 1975): 387–398.

Walch, Timothy. *Archives and Manuscripts: Security.* Chicago, 1977.

Weinstein, Robert S. and Larry Booth. *Collection, Use and Care of Historical Photographs.* Nashville, 1977.